ALEXANDER GEORGE WARD

AYAHUASCA
JUNGLE VISIONS
a coloring book

DIVINE
ARTS

Published by DIVINE ARTS

DivineArtsMedia.com

An imprint of Michael Wiese Productions

12400 Ventura Blvd. #1111

Studio City, CA 91604

(818) 379-8799, (818) 986-3408 (FAX)

Cover and interior design: Alexander George Ward

Editor: Gary Sunshine

Printed by McNaughton & Gunn, Inc., Saline, Michigan

Manufactured in the United States of America

Printed on Recycled Stock

This book belongs to

....

Hola!

My name is Alexander George Ward.

Welcome to my coloring book inspired by my time living
in the Amazon Jungle, studying the old Shamanic ways.

I hope I managed to capture a small part of the magic
I received in the jungle.

Within this coloring book you will find pages ranging in
levels of complexity and detail for colorers of all abilities.

If at any time you feel lost, know that all you need do
is color one empty space at a time.

At the back of this book you will find a Color Protector Page.
Tear this page out and place under the page you're coloring
so that marker pens won't bleed through to the other illustrations.

There need not be any rules here.
So pick any color and flow with the current of this book.

If you wish to share your colored creations
please do so at:
www.ayajungle.com

Or connect with me on social media:

 @ayajungle    @wardyworks   @wardyworks

DIVINE
ARTS

Interconnected

We are all interconnected
in symbiotic relationship
to the living, breathing,
self-regulating organism
we call Earth.

We must protect that
which creates and sustains
life on Earth.

Mother Nature,
Pachamama.

DIVINE
ARTS

Ayahuasca Jungle Visions   Alexander George Ward

Gratitude

To the cultures that survived
for thousands of years
by living in harmony with nature:

Thank you for keeping the ancient knowledge alive.

DIVINE
ARTS

Ayahuasca Jungle Visions   Alexander George Ward

Mountain Origins

The Amazon River,
source of the greatest abundance of life on Earth,
begins its life as a humble trickle of water
high up in the Andes Mountains of Peru.

DIVINE
ARTS

The Mighty Amazon River

That humble trickle of water
stretches four thousand miles to become
the mighty Amazon River.

It is the lifeblood of the world's largest rainforest,
the Amazon basin.

The healthy lungs of the Planet,
producing much of the Earth's oxygen.

It is responsible for an abundance of life.

DIVINE
ARTS

Down River

It is here I sail
down thinning streams
into thickening darkness.

A place where the stars shine with
a bright luminosity.

DIVINE
ARTS

Jungle Eyes

Entering a dense land so foreign,
at first so intimidating.

Frightened by the lights reflecting off
countless watching eyes in the jungle flora.

Paw Prints

Journeying deeper into the unknown.
On alert for danger everywhere.

DIVINE
ARTS

Cat Protector

The Amazon is home
to some of the world's most dangerous animals.

DIVINE
ARTS

Scales

But they have a beauty that can't be ignored.
All with different patterned coats
and colors galore!

Canopy of Life

An entire world lives up in the canopy.
Exotic sounds and chatter of life,
more than anywhere else on Earth.

A third of the world's birds live
up in the Amazon canopy.

The Plants Speak

The plants are alive and speak
to us of their healing properties.

Over a quarter of the medicine
used in the modern world
comes from the Amazon.

DIVINE
ARTS

Ancient Cultures

There are ancient cultures
that have kept their ears, hearts, and minds open
so they may hear what the plants have to share.

They know of plants to heal any ailment.

DIVINE
ARTS

Shamanic Underworld

The Amazon Jungle has been in existence
for at least 55 million years.

Below the visible surface
lies an ancient memory.

DIVINE
ARTS

Ayahuasca Jungle Visions   Alexander George Ward

Tribal Village

Human inhabitants first settled
the Amazon region
at least 11,200 years ago.

DIVINE
ARTS

Elders

Knowledge keepers of ancient ways.

Joy

Never give up looking for the beauty in life.

Play

Breathe

Dance

Play

Spread your wings of love in the light.

DIVINE
ARTS

Local Patterns

Cultures rich in embroidery art,
following the patterns of life.

Shipibo

Patterns from the Shipibo tradition.
Patterns that can be read like sheet music
to their ancient healing songs.

DIVINE
ARTS

Alexander George Ward

Ayahuasca Medicine

Ayahuasca is a sacred medicine
originating from ancient Amazonian tribes.
A brew created from mixing the *Banisteriopsis caapi* vine
and the *Psychotria viridis* leaf.

Together they create the mother of all medicine:
the Ayahuasca.

A sacred healing sacrament.

DIVINE
ARTS

Shaman

A Medicine Healer.
Learned in the ways of the Plant Teacher.

Ayahuasca is the clearest mirror imaginable,
showing what you may never have seen before:
who you truly are.

DIVINE
ARTS

Ayahuasca Ceremony

The sacred brew is given in ritual ceremony.
Guided by the Shaman
for the purposes of healing.

An altar houses the various different props
that get used through ceremony
for various ritual purposes.

DIVINE
ARTS

Smudging

Those participating in ceremony are smudged with incense.
Cleansing and purifying the energy.

DIVINE
ARTS

The Shaman & Ayahuasca

According to the ancient Amazon cultures,
Ayahuasca is used to access the Spirit world.

The translation of Ayahuasca is, after all,
"The Vine of Souls."

Icaro

The Shaman begins to sing their ancient healing songs,
the Icaros.

Learned from the Ayahuasca and Plant Spirits.
Songs to heal people of multitudes of problems
and to guide people deeper into the mystical experience.

Spirits

The Shaman calls in the Spirits to protect the sacred space.
Lessons of the Ayahuasca spring to life.

DIVINE
ARTS

Ancestors

A realm of Spirits and Ancestors
here to teach and assist.

Sacred songs passed through generations,
healing those who seek it.

DIVINE
ARTS

The Veil

Inner worlds full of light begin to unfold
beyond the lifting of the veil.
The Kingdom within.

DIVINE
ARTS

Self Recognizing Self

Sparks of recognition that what you see
behind the eyes of another
is just another you.

Awakening the eye that sees past the illusion of separateness
to see the divine consciousness in all.

DIVINE
ARTS

Unbound Consciousness

Consciousness broadens to encompass surrounding life.

To feel the wind in the feathers of a hawk,
the sticking power of a toad's foot,
the strength of a snake's muscles,
its scales glistening in fluctuating colors.

DIVINE
ARTS

Symbiosis

No separation between life and the environment around it.
It is all one movement.

The hummingbird lives in symbiosis with its environment.

DIVINE
ARTS

Evolve

There are no boundaries to Nature's creativity.

Oneness

Oneness does not exist within the abstraction of a thought.
It is a very real quality to life that can only be
experienced by being felt personally in this very present moment.

DIVINE
ARTS

Release

All the negative emotion you've unknowingly picked up
and held on to all these years
Ayahuasca purges from your very being.
Shed like old skin.

DIVINE
ARTS

Made of Stardust

To look at life
as a conscious element of the universe.
Knowing that what you see
is yourself.

You are the unfolding universe itself.

DIVINE
ARTS

Energy

DIVINE
ARTS

You are the life energy
that flows within all.

What began as one
is now everything you see.

Flow

Let everything flow through you.
Forgive, release, and breathe.

Just be present.

DIVINE
ARTS

Death

You are the Eternal Self.
Experiencing the variety of life.

Heal Thyself

To heal yourself is to heal your ancestors,
your lineage.

So let the way of the heart shine through.

Set free all those who came before
and all those who will come after.

DIVINE
ARTS

Flower of Life

Pattern of creation.

Modernity

Life out of balance.

DIVINE
ARTS

Ayahuasca Jungle Visions   Alexander George Ward

Eternal Tribe

Paradise is no place,
it is a state of being.

Learn to be present with the paradise within.

Nature

Four thousand miles from its origin,
the Amazon River ends its journey
into the Atlantic Ocean.

It's no coincidence that in this time
of great ecological uncertainty,
Ayahuasca and knowledge of the ancient ways
take flight out of the jungle
and help us repair our connection to nature.

DIVINE
ARTS

Ayahuasca Jungle Visions   Alexander George Ward

Pachamama

From the root of the Amazon
the great life-giver of the Planet,
the embodiment of the Spirit Pachamama.

May we awaken to its infinite beauty, love, and grace.

DIVINE
ARTS

Ayahuasca Jungle Visions   Alexander George Ward

Index

01
Ayahuasca Jungle Visions

02
Hola!

03
Interconnected

04
Gratitude

05
Mountain Origins

06
The Mighty Amazon River

07
Down River

08
Jungle Eyes

09
Paw Prints

10
Cat Protector

11
Scales

12
Canopy of Life

Index

13
The Plants Speak

14
Ancient Cultures

15
Shamanic Underworld

16
Tribal Village

17
Elders

18
Joy

19
Play

20
Local Patterns

21
Shipibo

22
Ayahuasca Medicine

23
Shaman

24
Ayahuasca Ceremony

Index

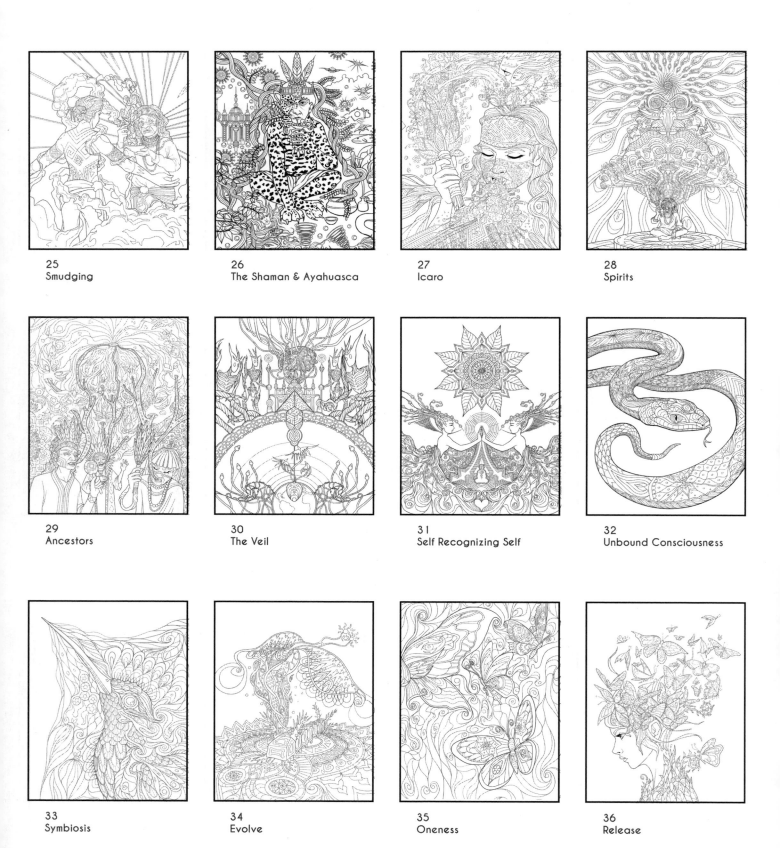

25
Smudging

26
The Shaman & Ayahuasca

27
Icaro

28
Spirits

29
Ancestors

30
The Veil

31
Self Recognizing Self

32
Unbound Consciousness

33
Symbiosis

34
Evolve

35
Oneness

36
Release

Index

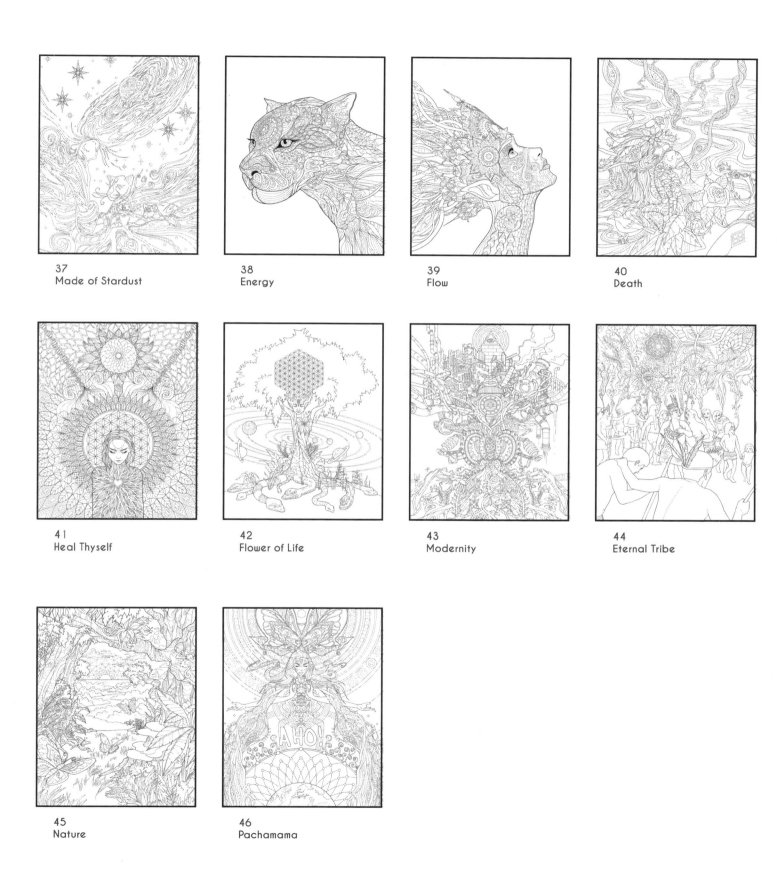

37
Made of Stardust

38
Energy

39
Flow

40
Death

41
Heal Thyself

42
Flower of Life

43
Modernity

44
Eternal Tribe

45
Nature

46
Pachamama

ERNST HAECKEL

INCREDIBLE
LIFE FORMS

— A Coloring Book —

Also from
Divine Arts
ERNST HAECKEL
Engravings

Celebrating the sacred in everyday life

THE SHAMAN & AYAHUASCA
Journeys to Sacred Realms
DON JOSÉ CAMPOS

Internationally respected Peruvian shaman Don José Campos introduces the practices and benefits of Ayahuasca, the psychoactive plant brew used for healing by Amazonian shamans for as long as 70,000 years. Called a plant teacher because it can heal physical, psychological, and emotional blocks, Ayahuasca takes the patient to other realms and dimensions, providing profound insight into our true nature and place in the cosmos.

"This remarkable book suggests a path back to understanding the profound healing and spiritual powers that are here for us in the plant world, reawakening our respect for the natural world, and thus for ourselves."
— **John Robbins, author of** *Diet for a New America*

$16.95 · 144 PAGES · ORDER #SHAMANBK · ISBN 9781611250039

Transforming self. Celebrating life.

Divine Arts was created five years ago to share some of the new and ancient knowledge that is rapidly emerging from the indigenous and wisdom cultures of the world; and to present new voices that express eternal truths in innovative and accessible ways.

We have realized from the shifts in our own consciousness that millions of people worldwide are simultaneously expanding their awareness and experiencing the multi-dimensional nature of reality.

Our authors, masters and teachers from around the world, have come together from all spiritual practices to create Divine Arts books. Our unity comes in celebrating the sacredness of life, and having the intention that our work will assist in raising our consciousness which will ultimately benefit all sentient beings.

We trust that these books will serve you on whatever path you journey, and we welcome hearing from you.

Michael Wiese and Geraldine Overton,
Publishers

mw@mwp.com   *glow@blue-earth.co.uk*

DIVINE ARTS | DIVINEARTSMEDIA.COM

ALEXANDER GEORGE WARD

AYAHUASCA
JUNGLE VISIONS
a coloring book

COLOR PROTECTOR PAGE

Tear out this page and place under the page
you're coloring so that marker pens
won't bleed through to the other illustrations.

Pencil crayons are great for achieving soft, blended colors and tones.

Marker pens are great for achieving a bold, striking look.

For more tips on coloring techniques please visit:

www.ayajungle.com

DIVINE
ARTS